# Vintage Retro Adult Coloring Book

## *This Coloring book belongs to:*

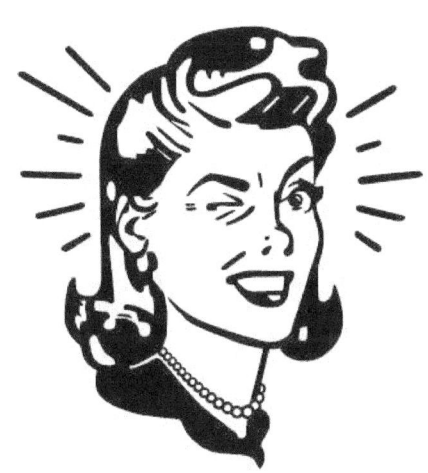

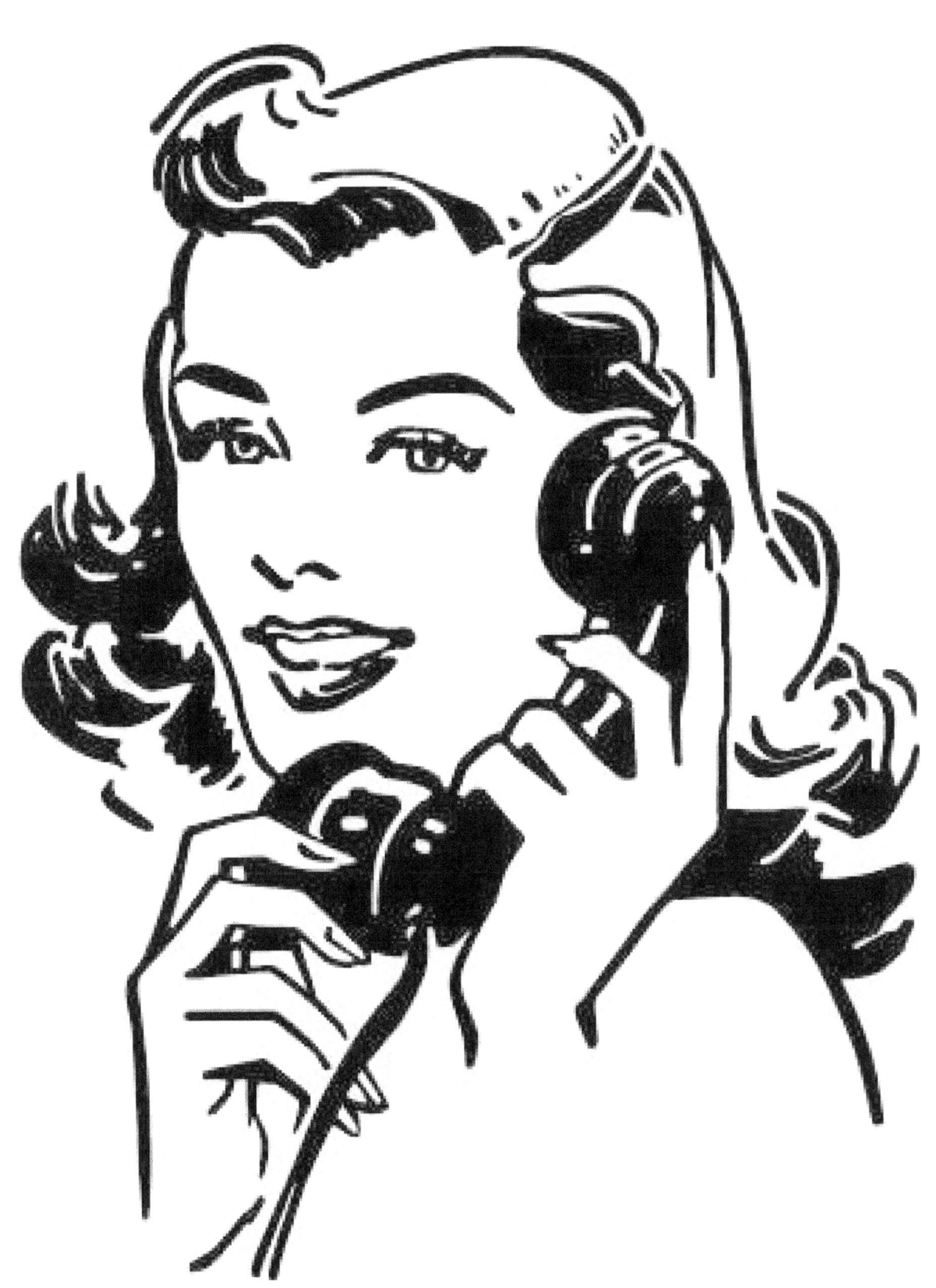

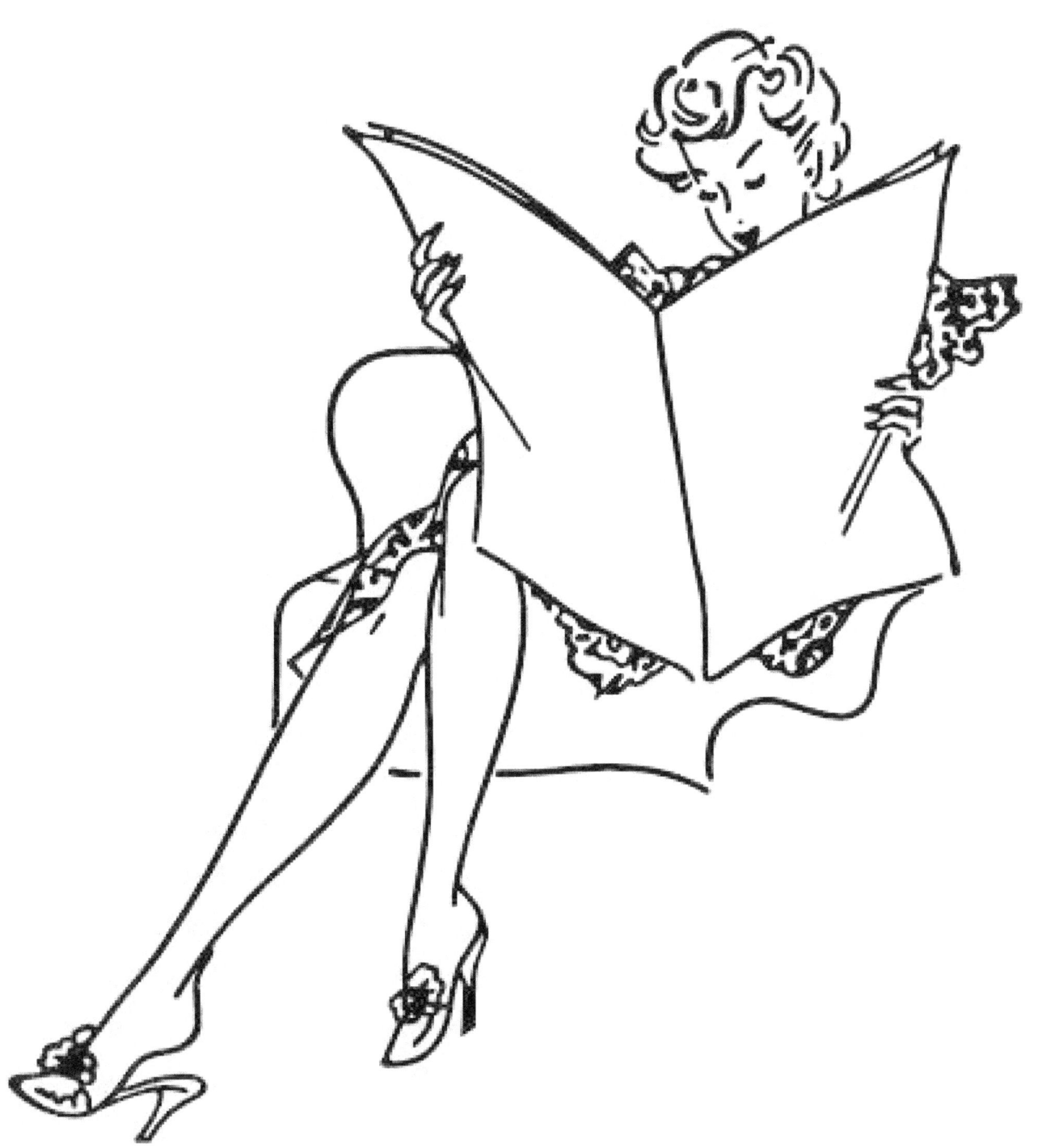

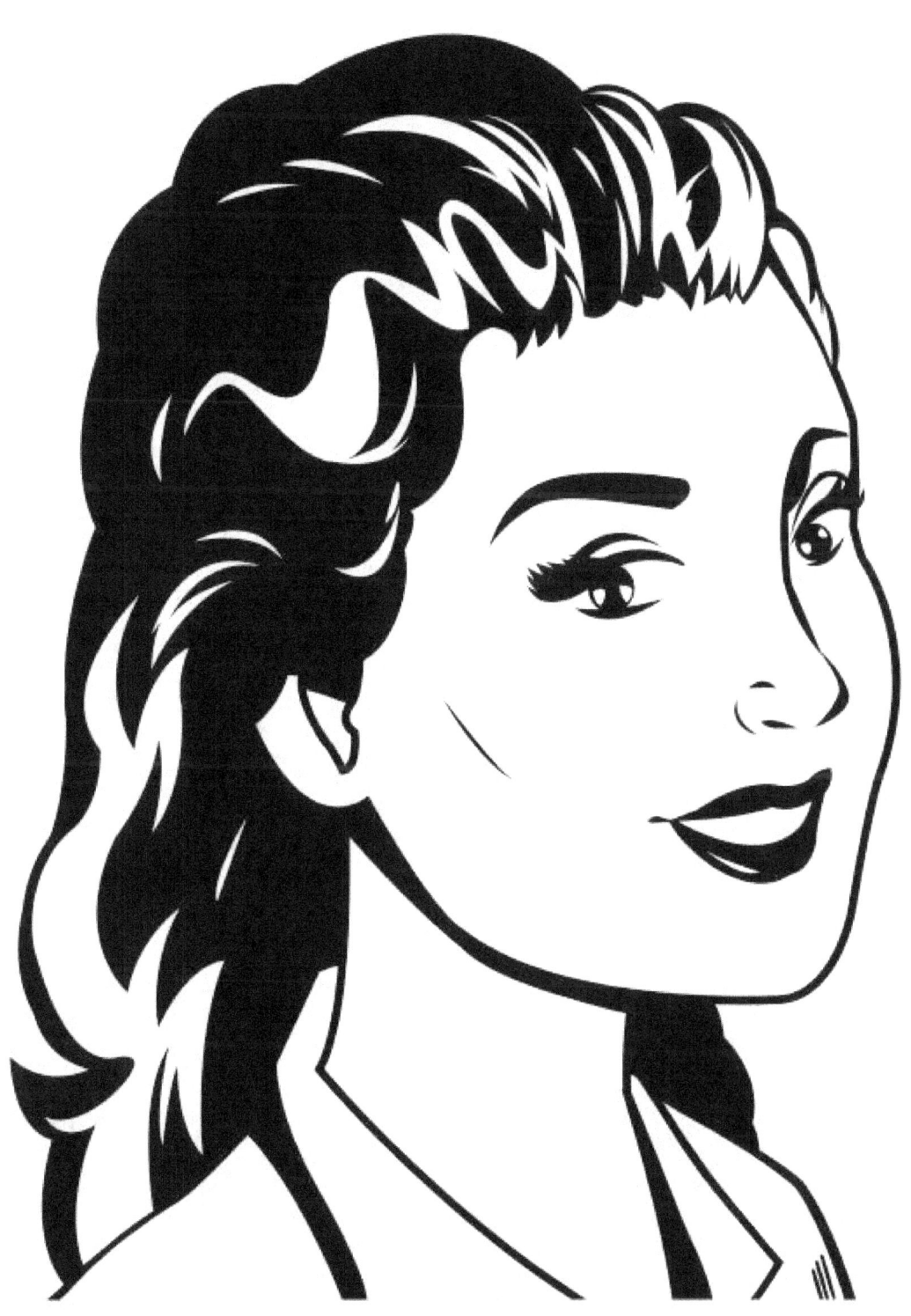

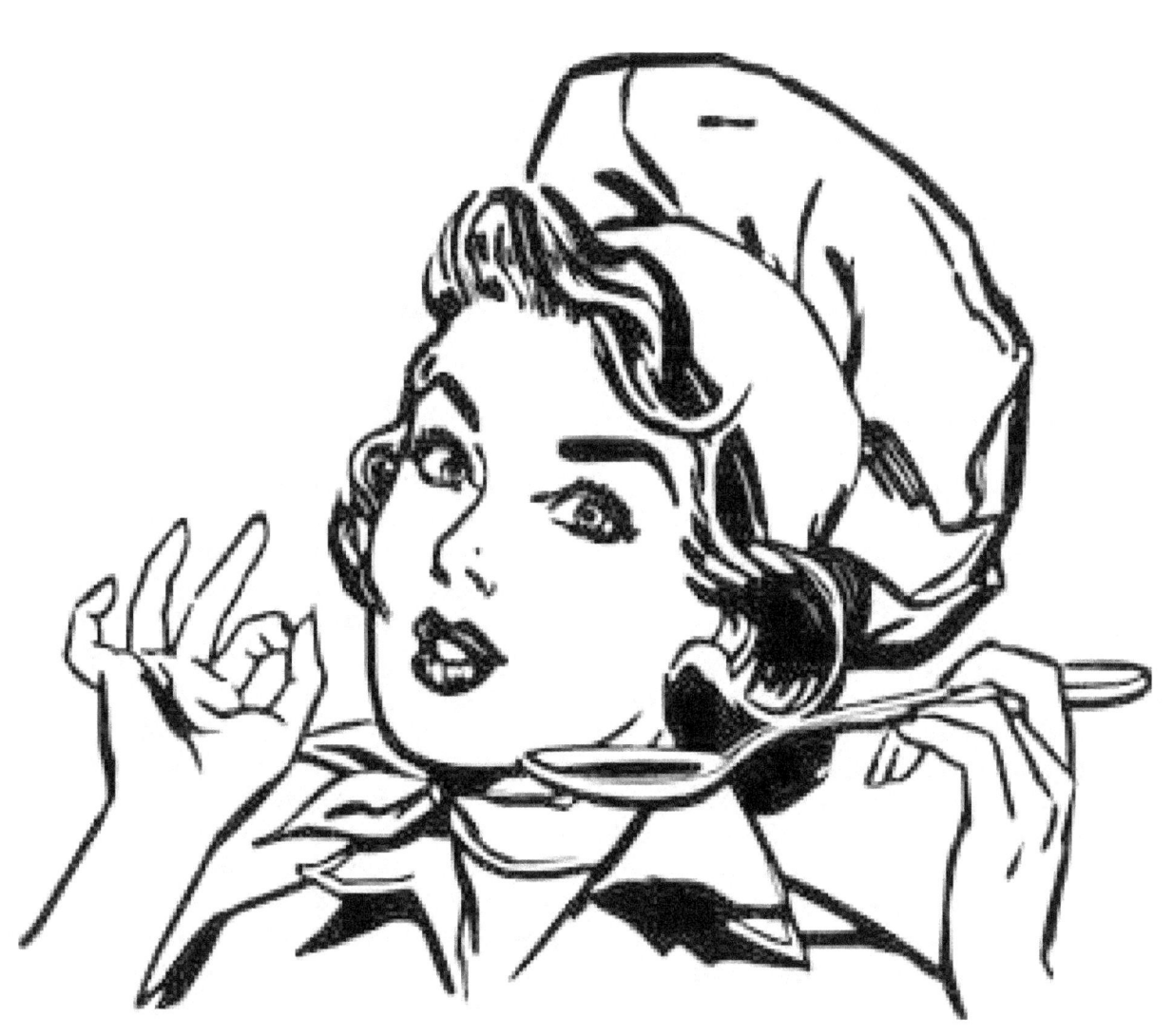

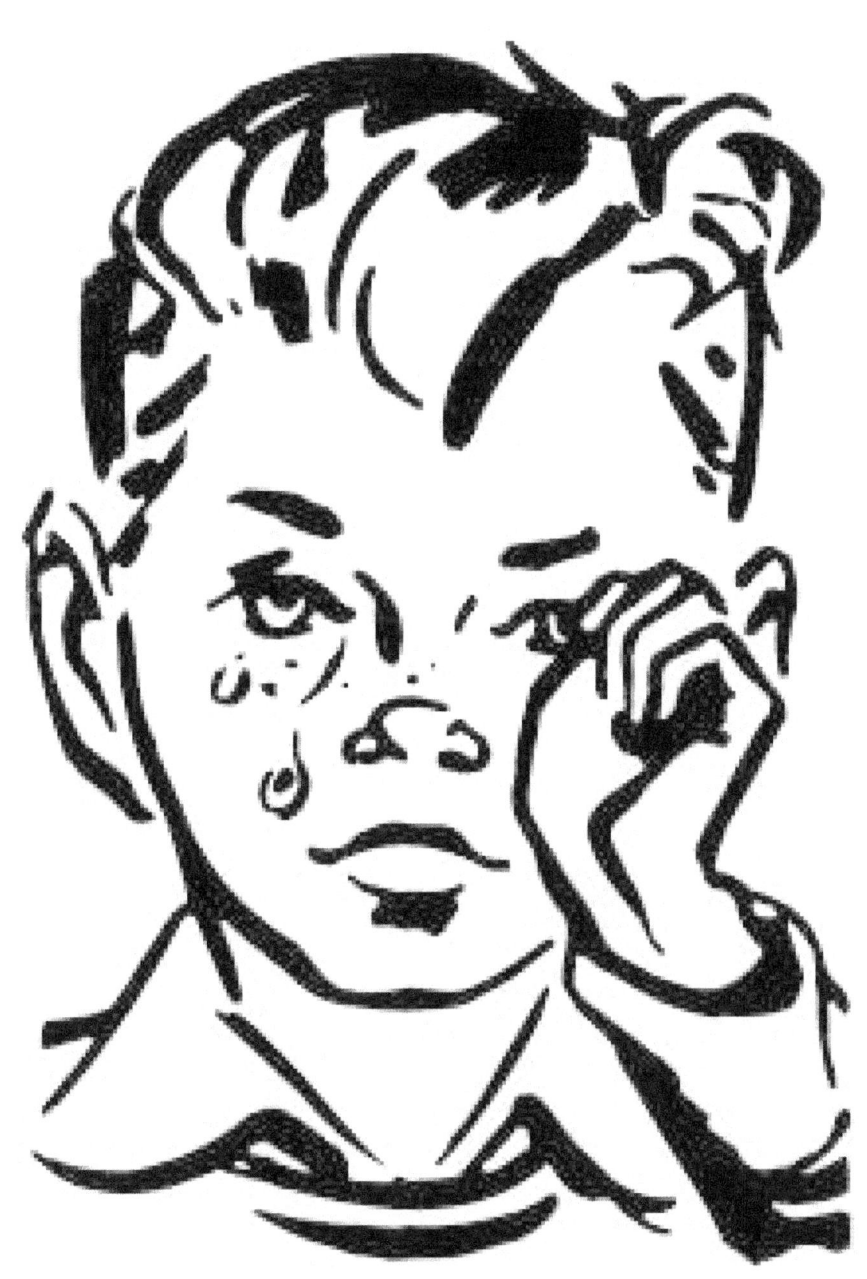

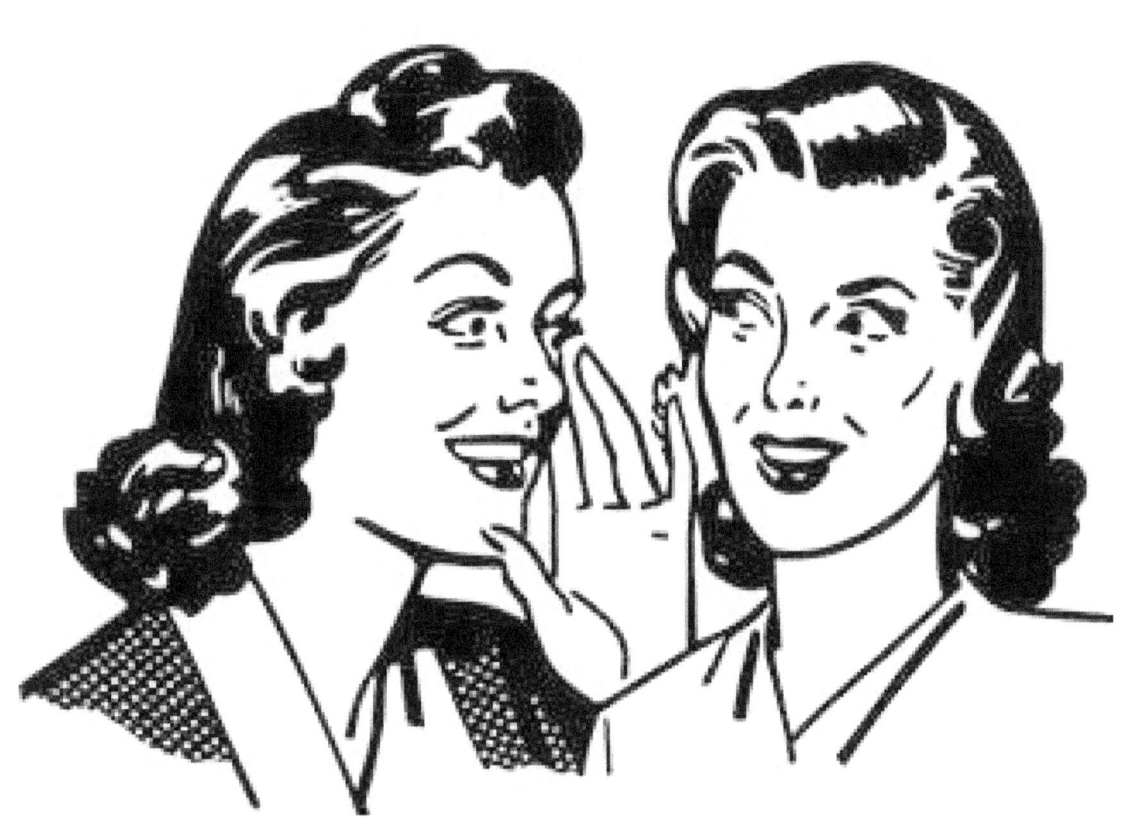

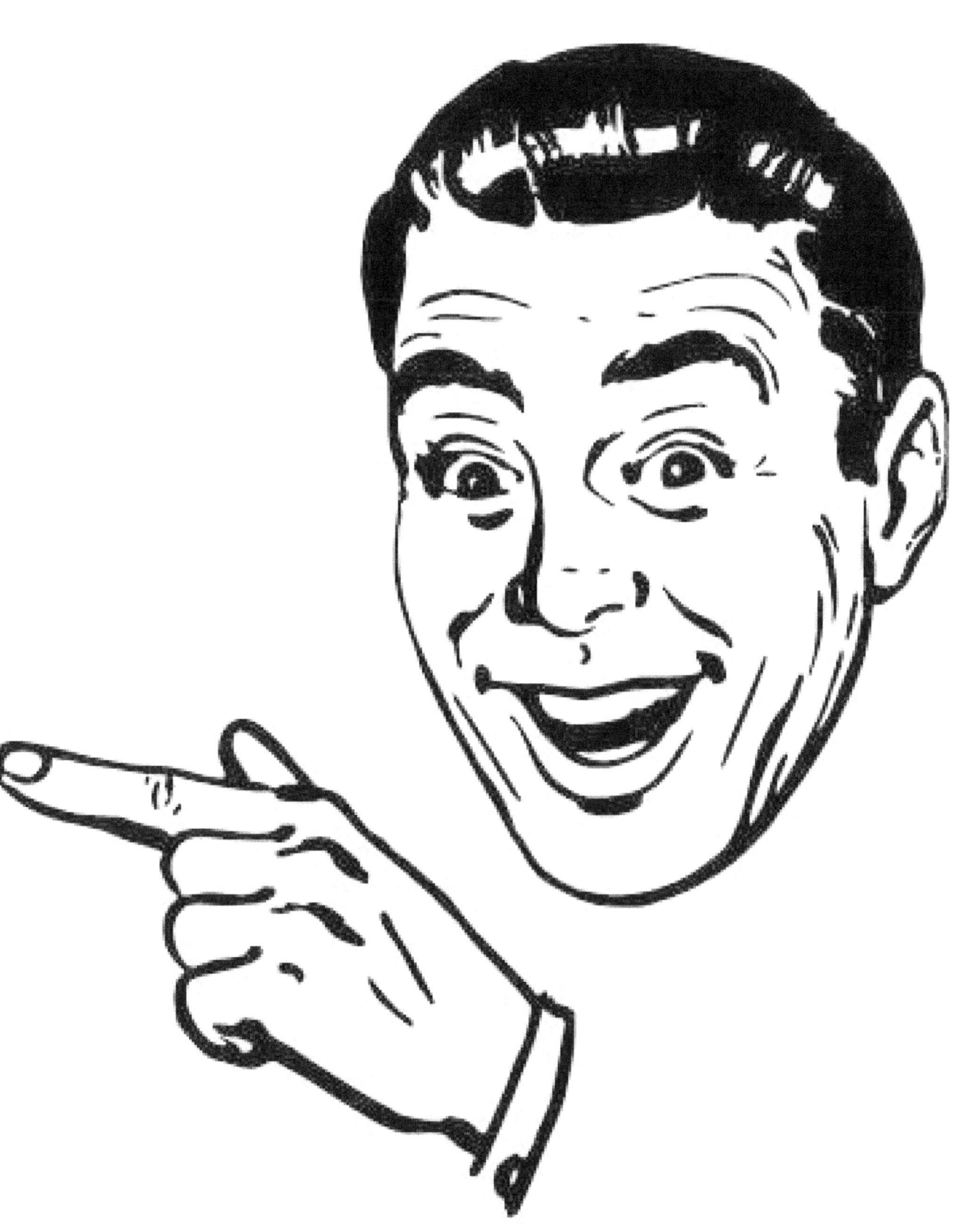

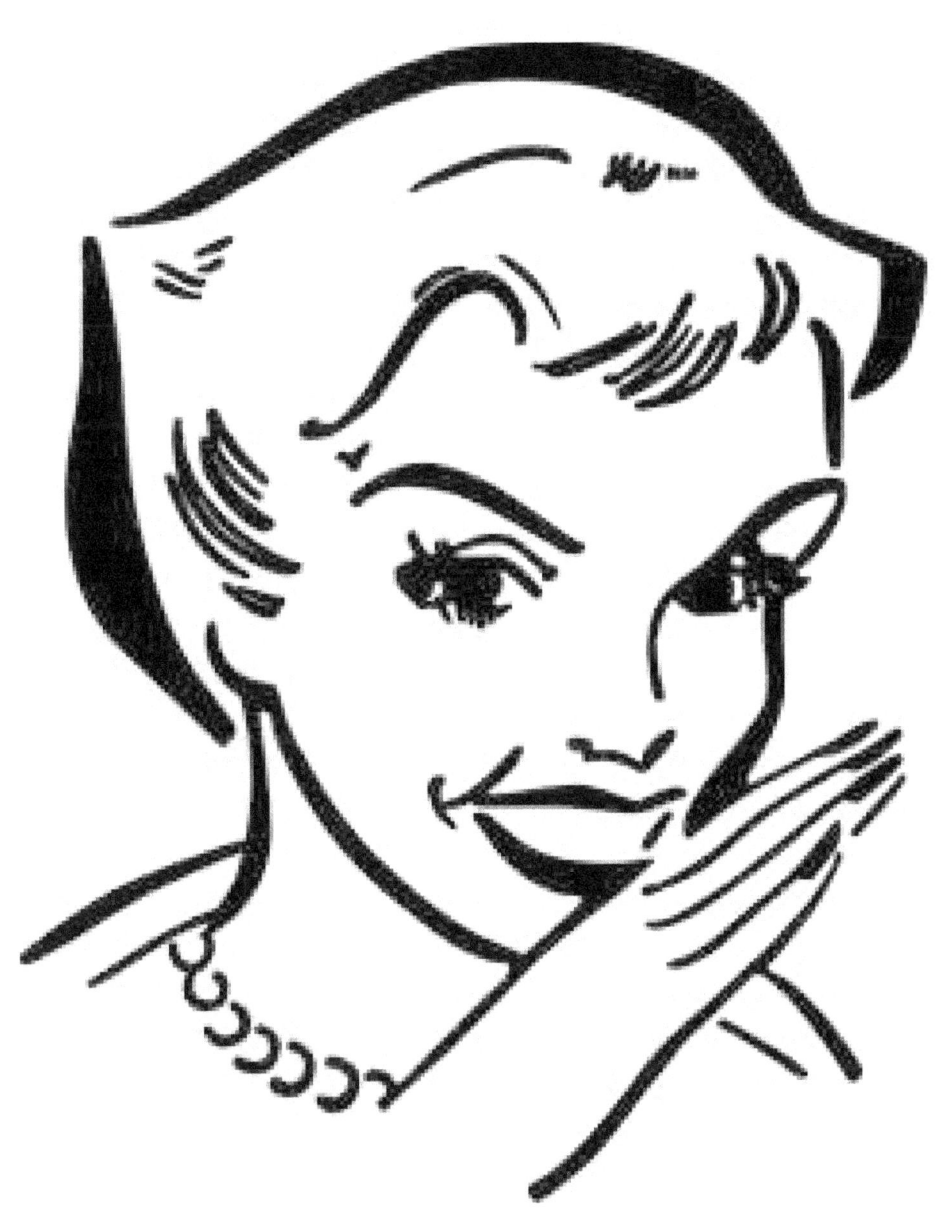

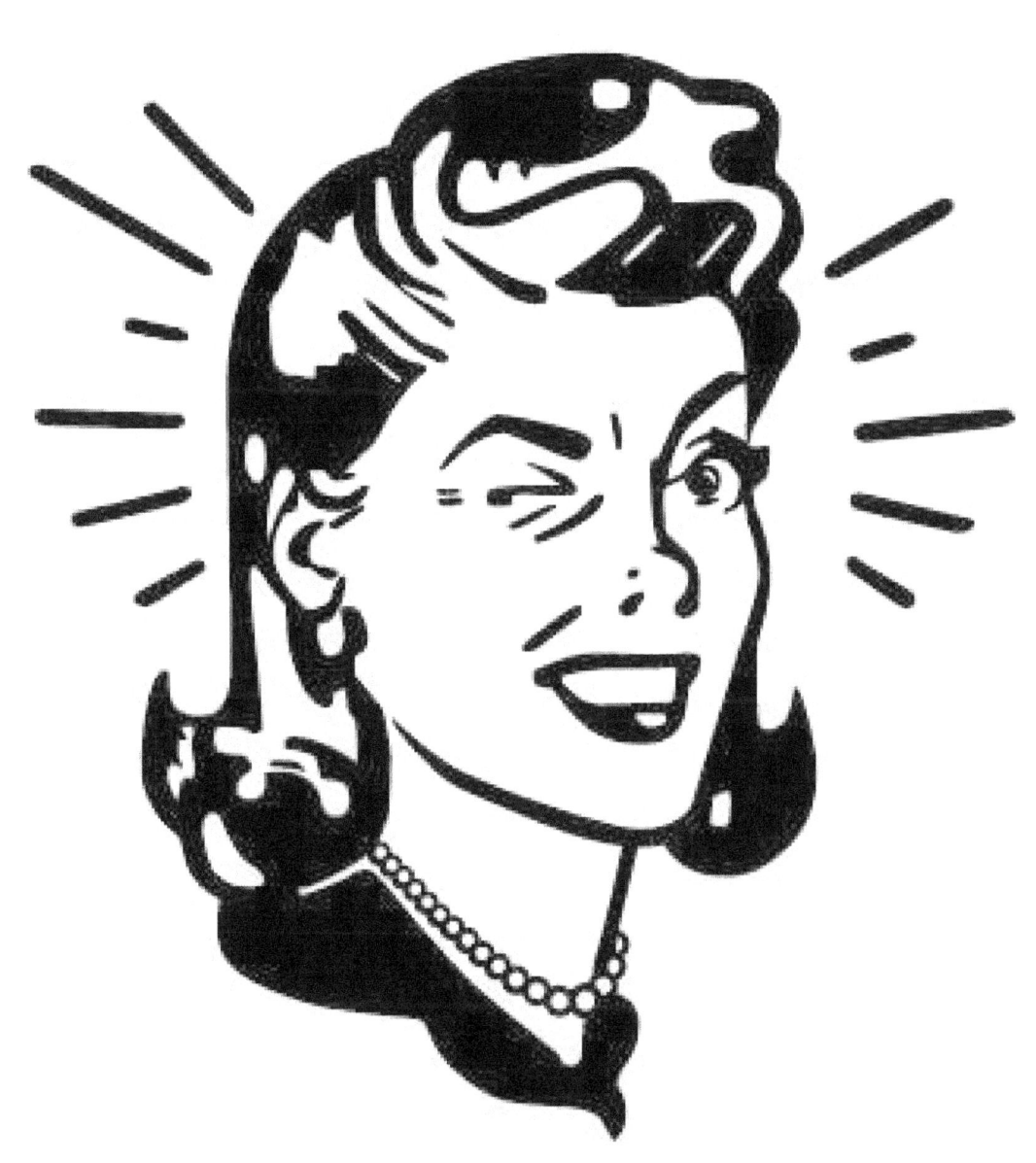

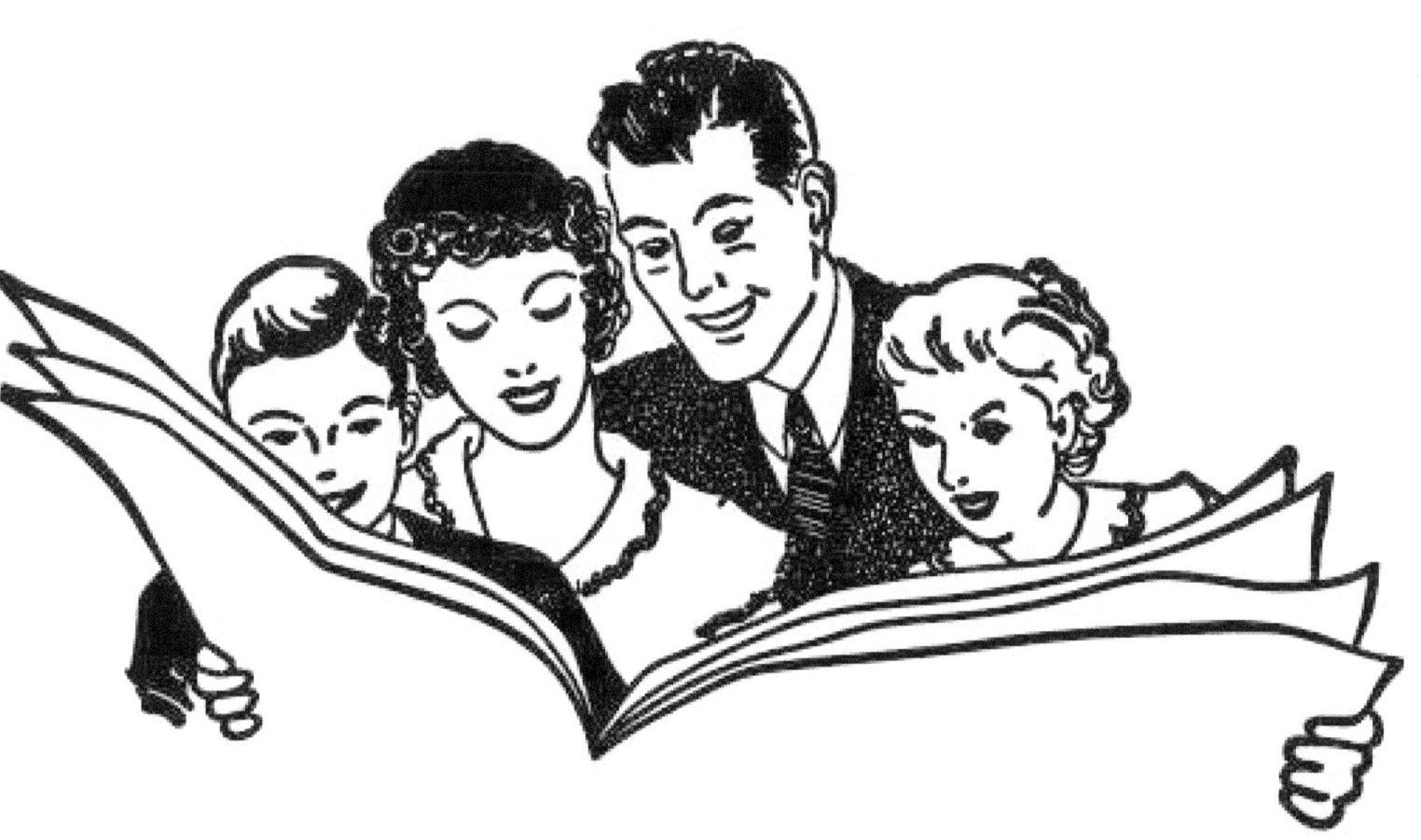

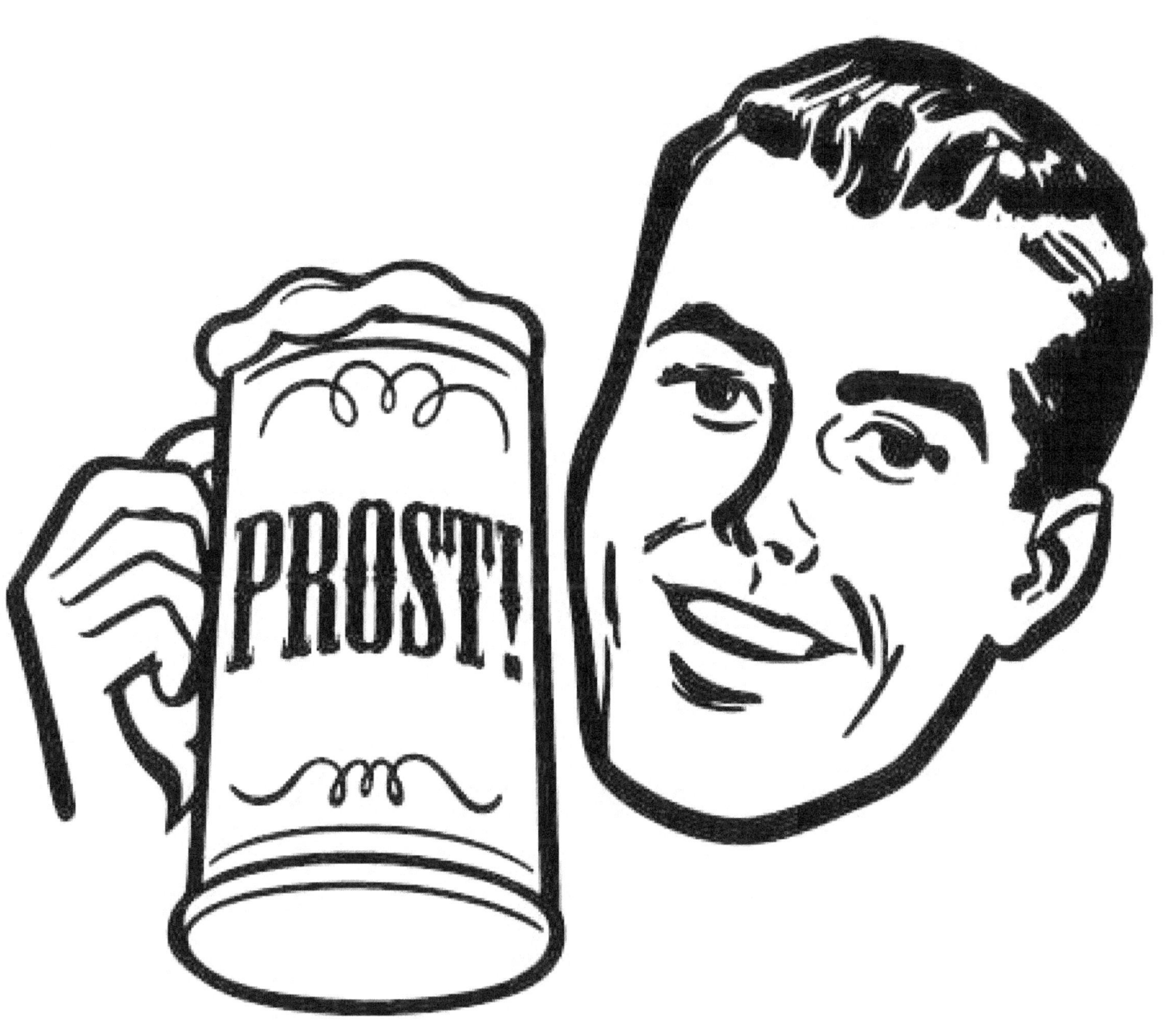

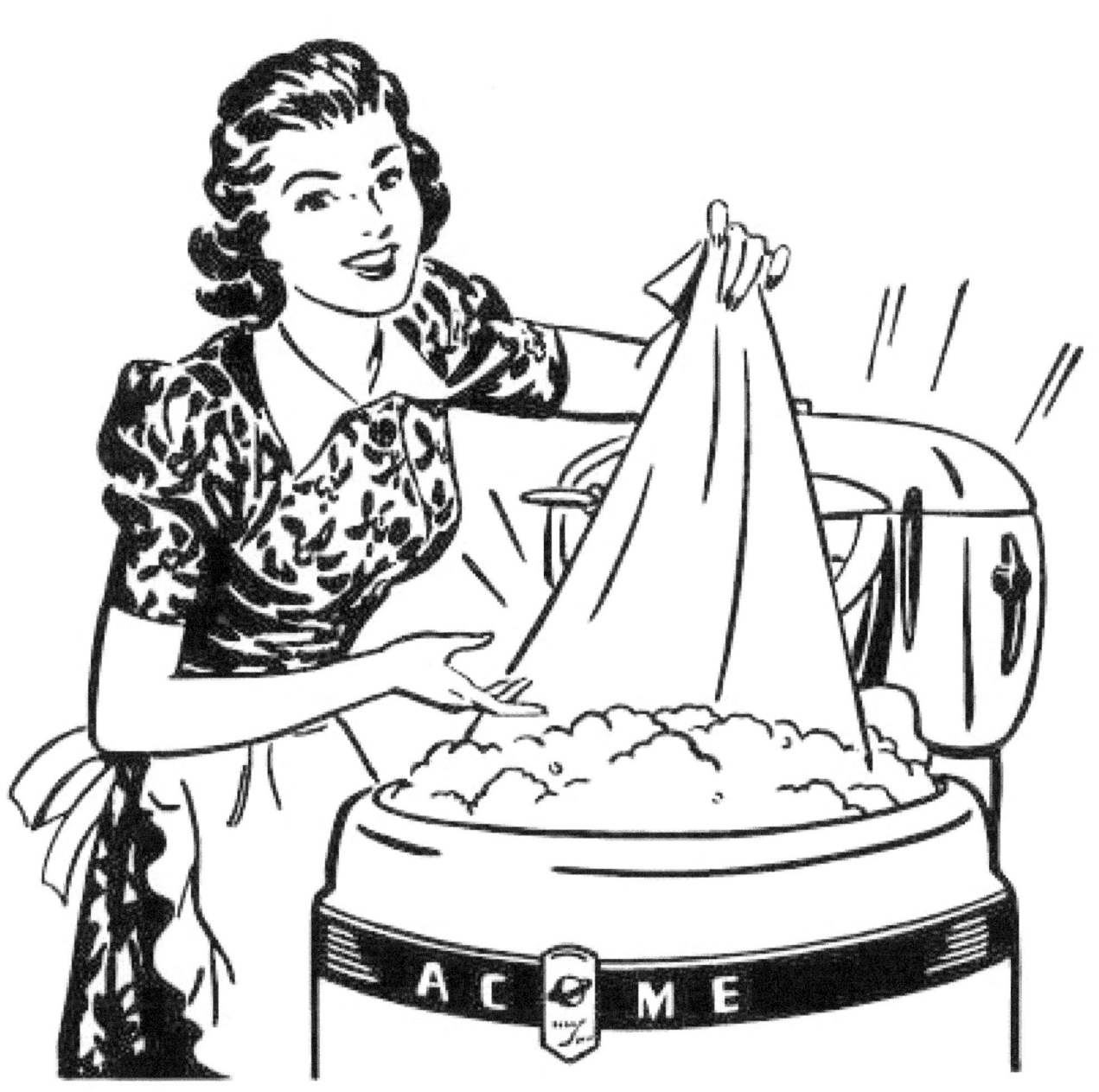

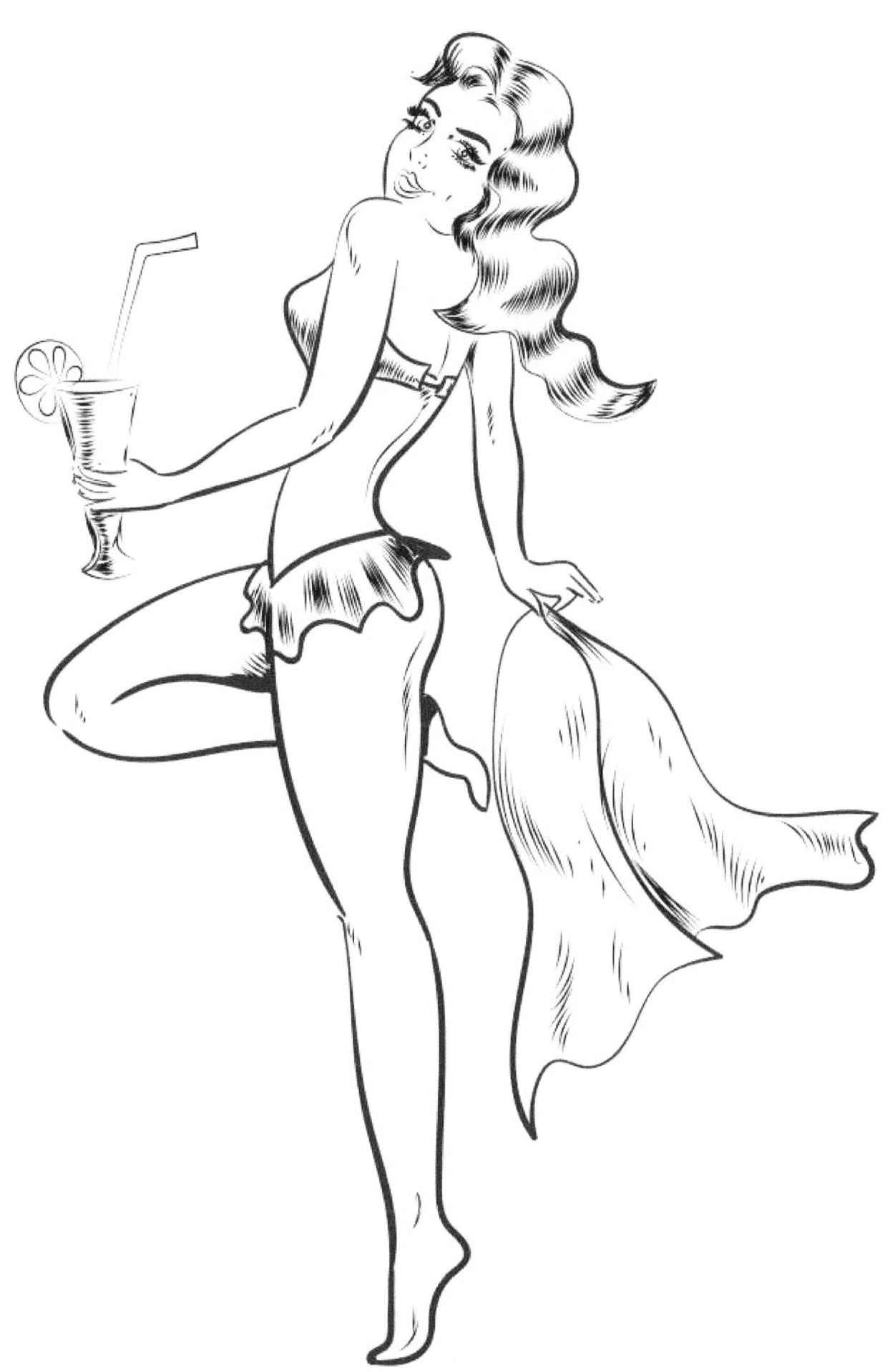

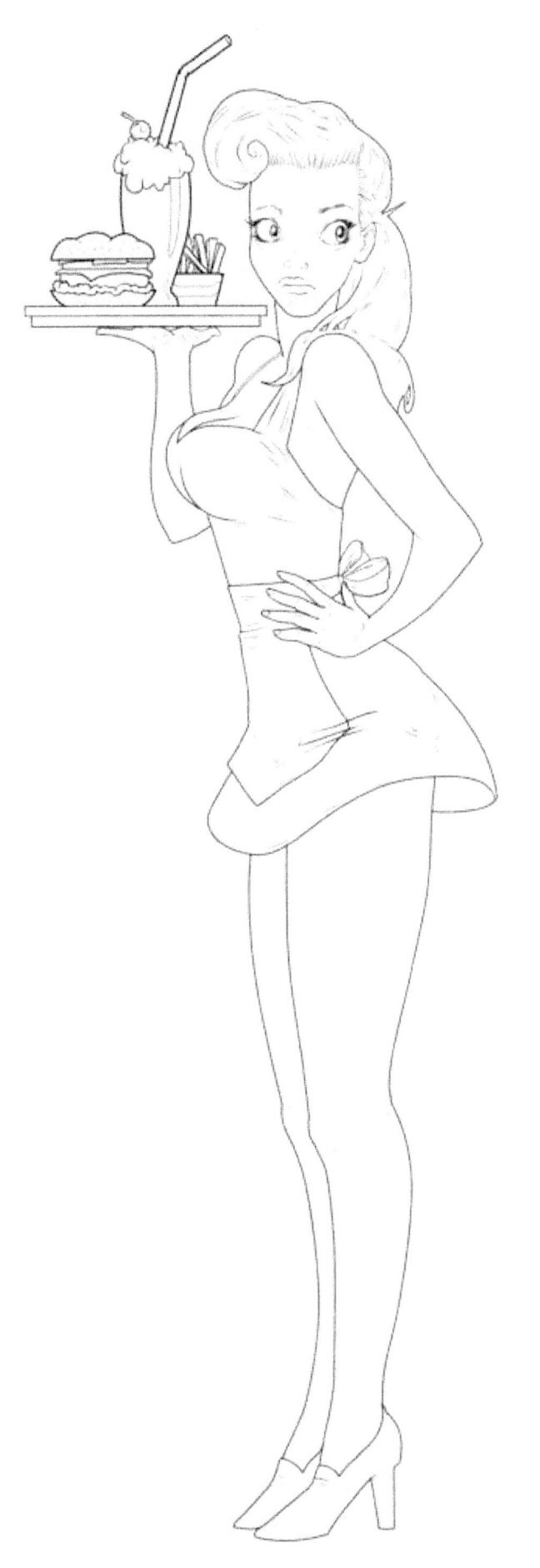

Surprise Bonus Beautiful Faces Coloring Pages to Enjoy.

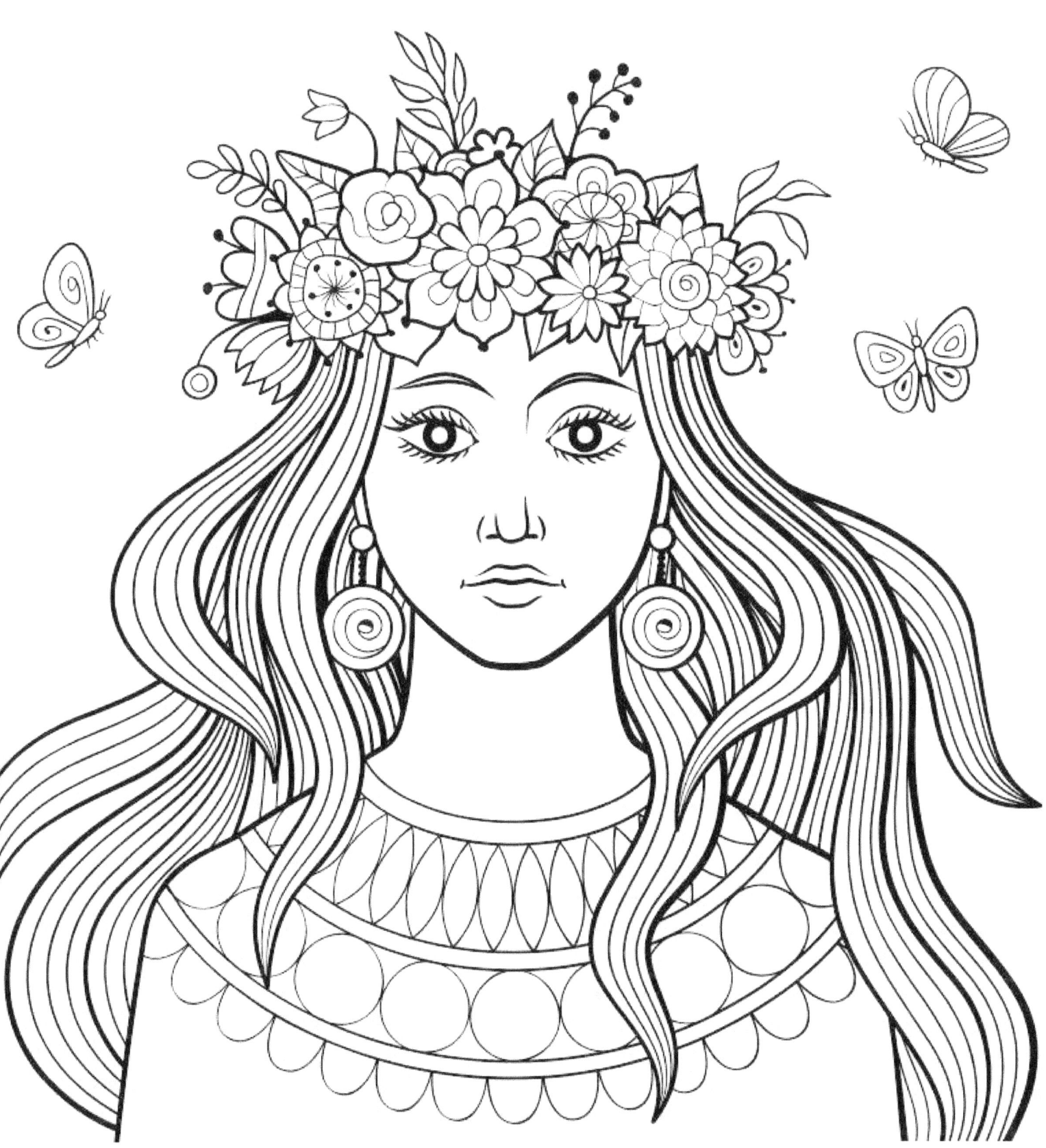

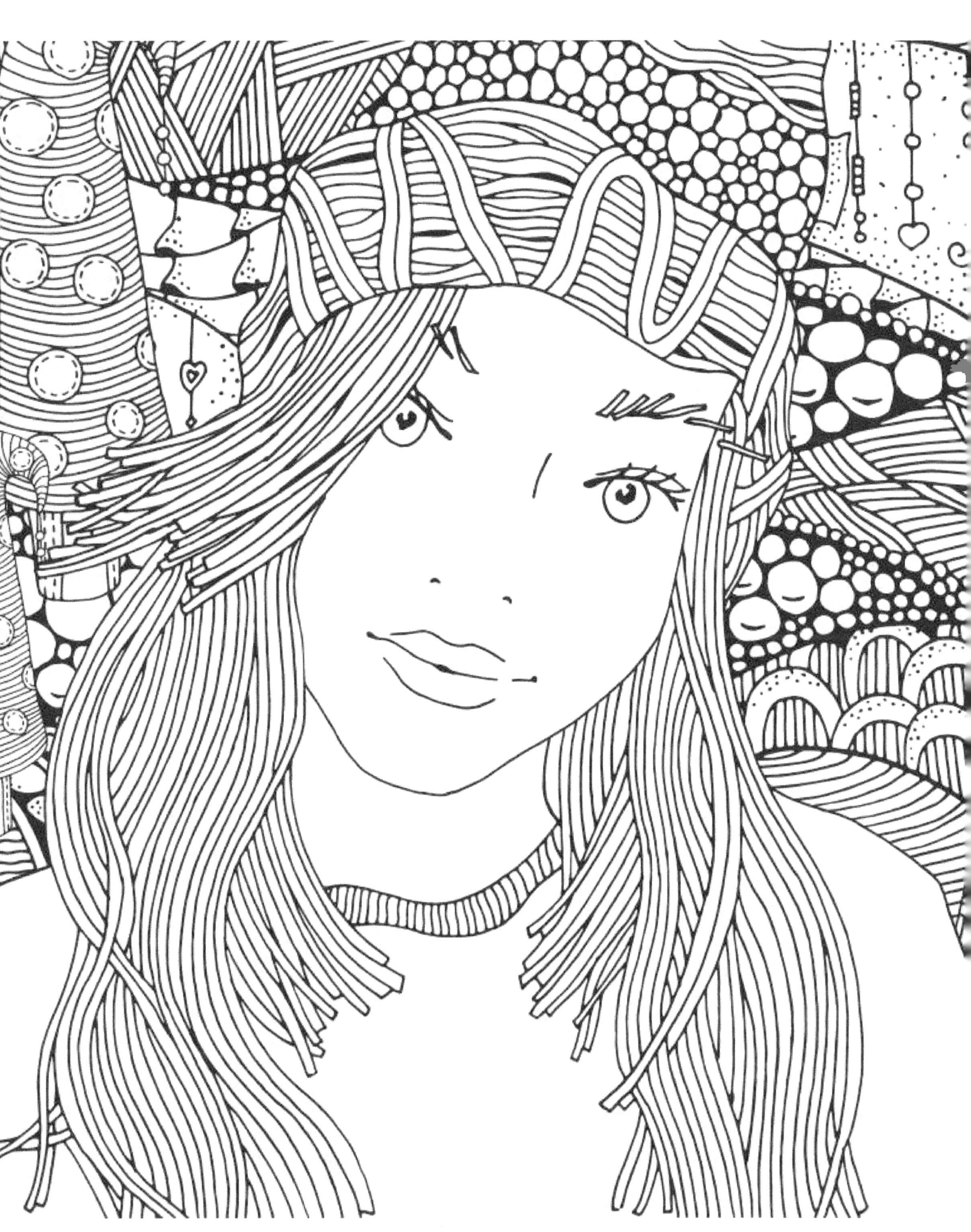

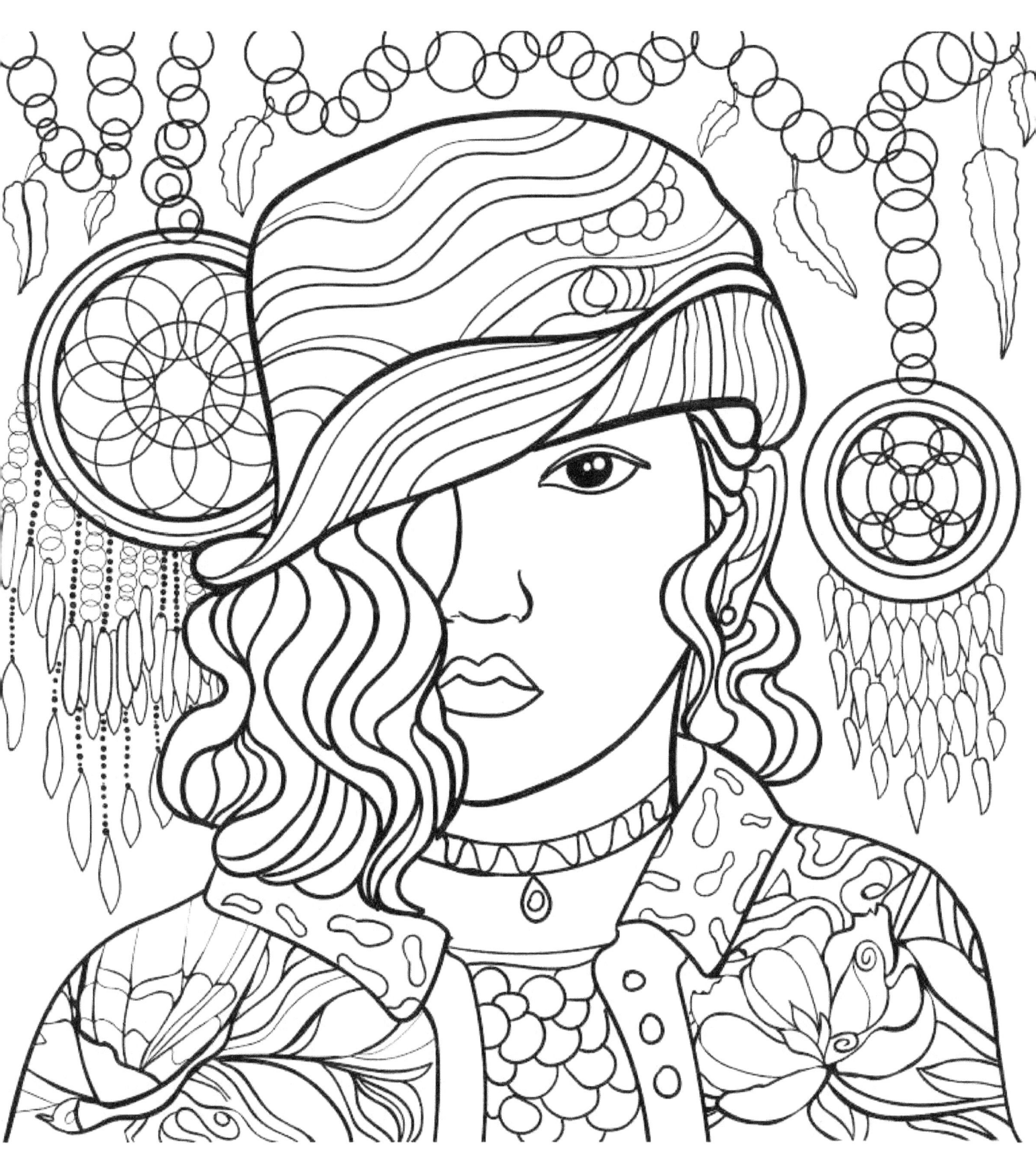

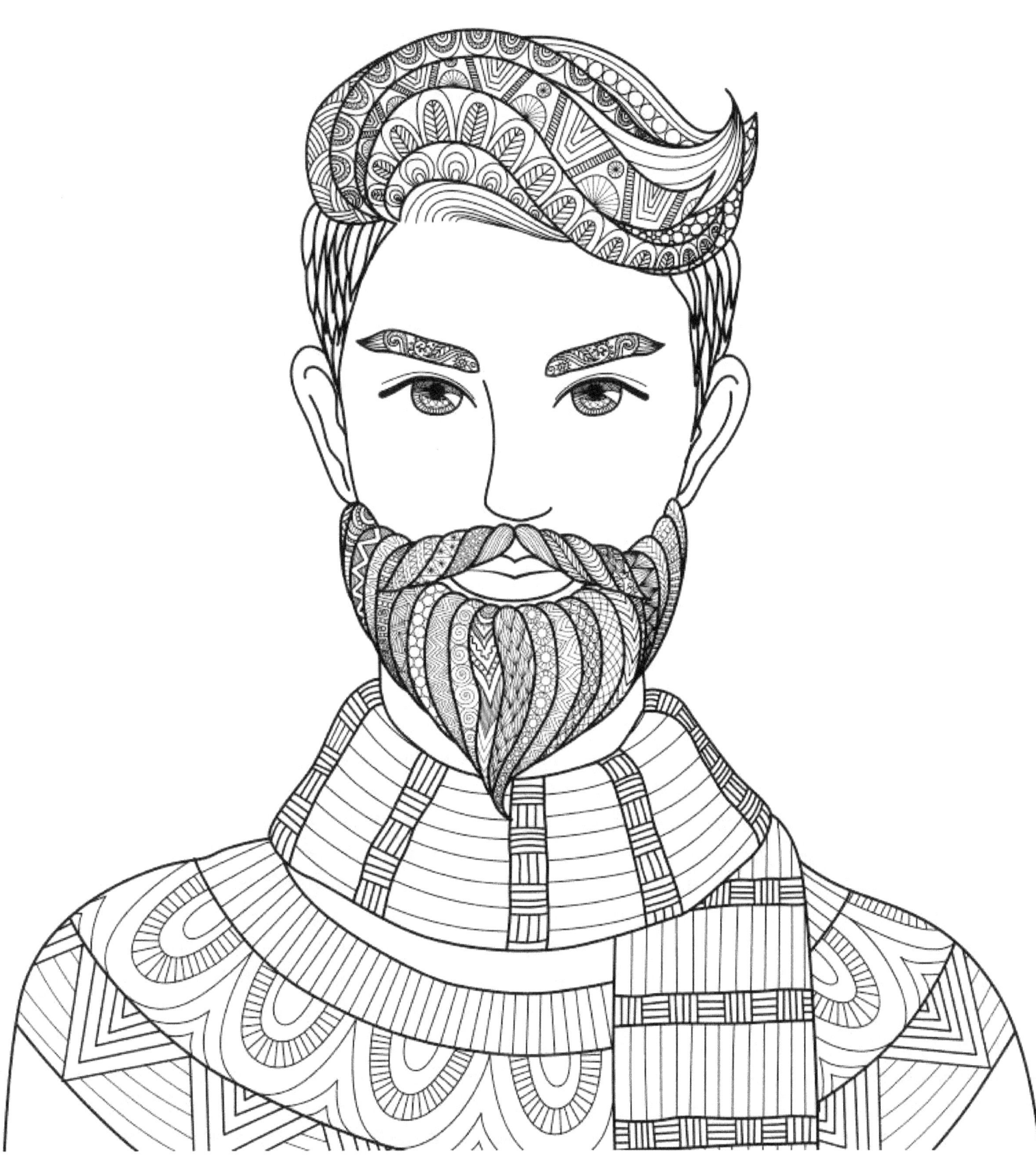

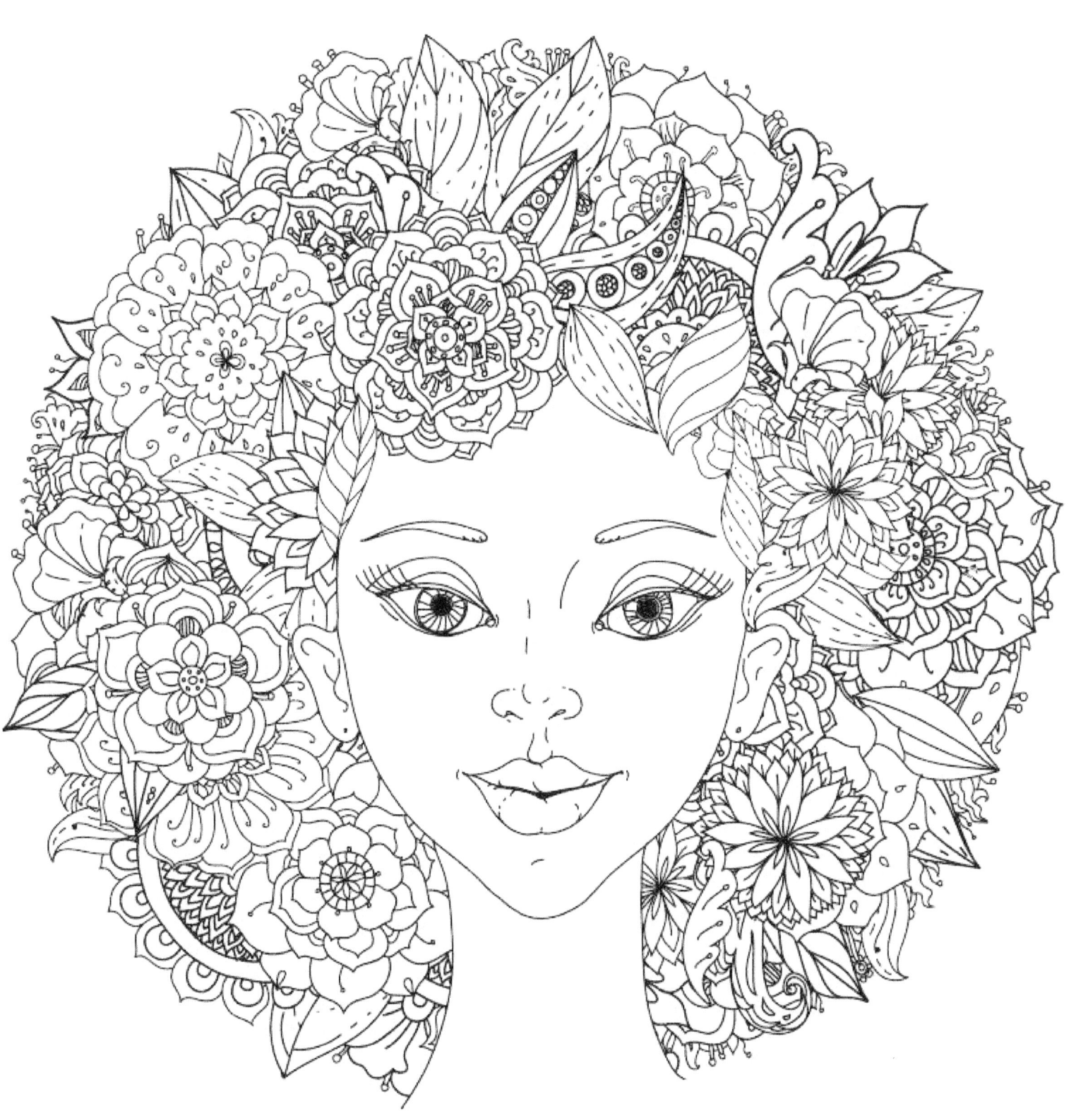

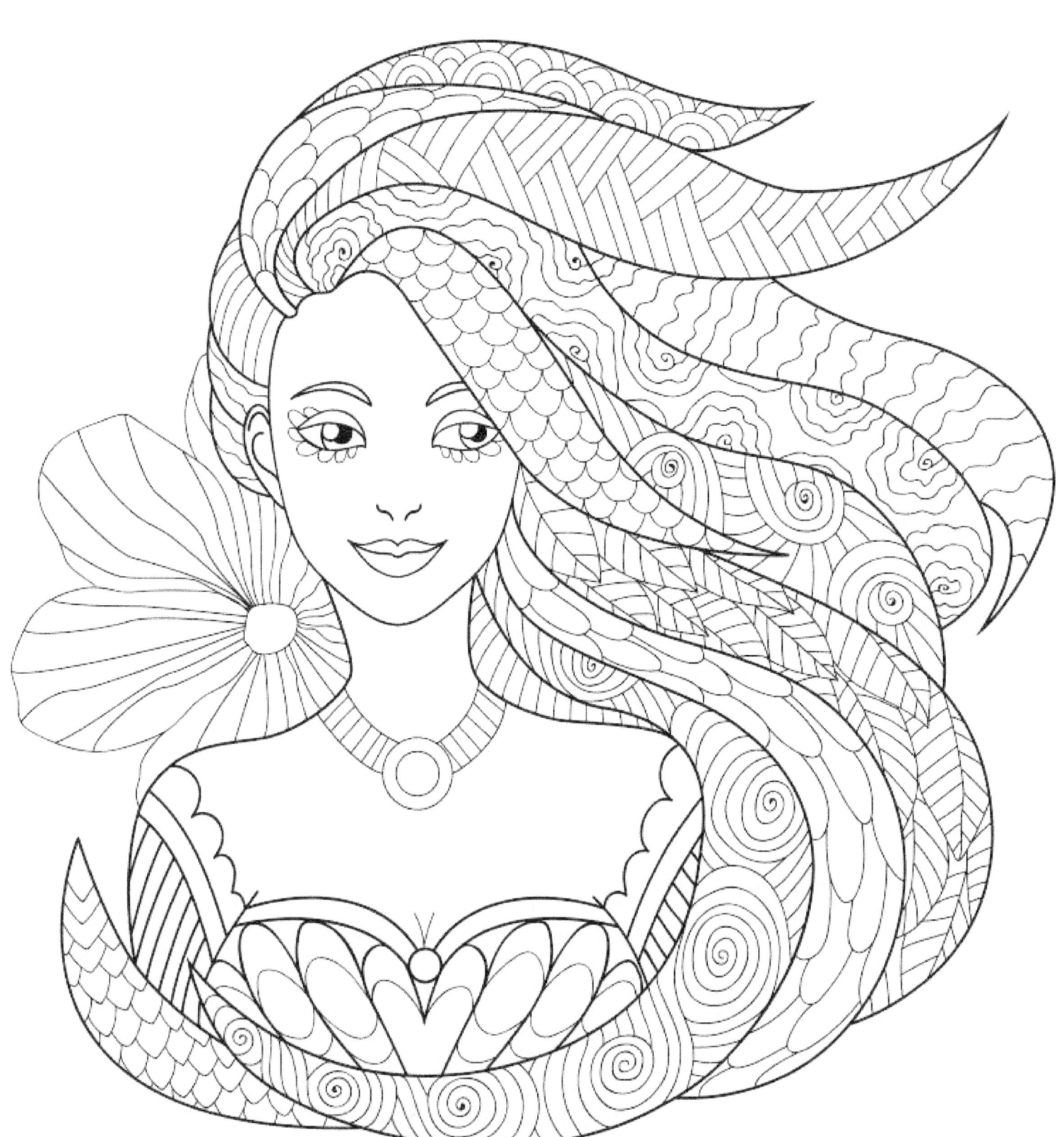

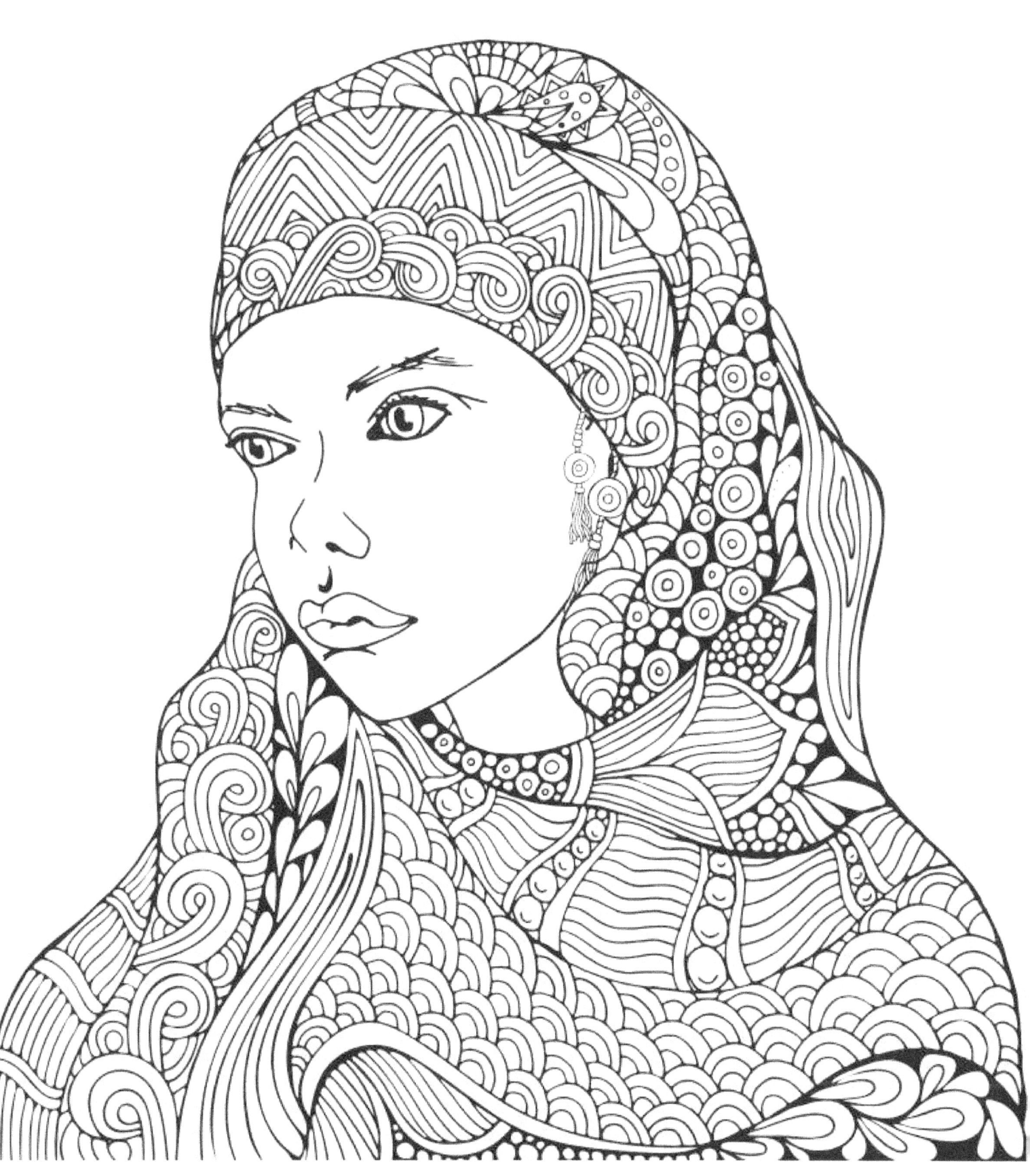

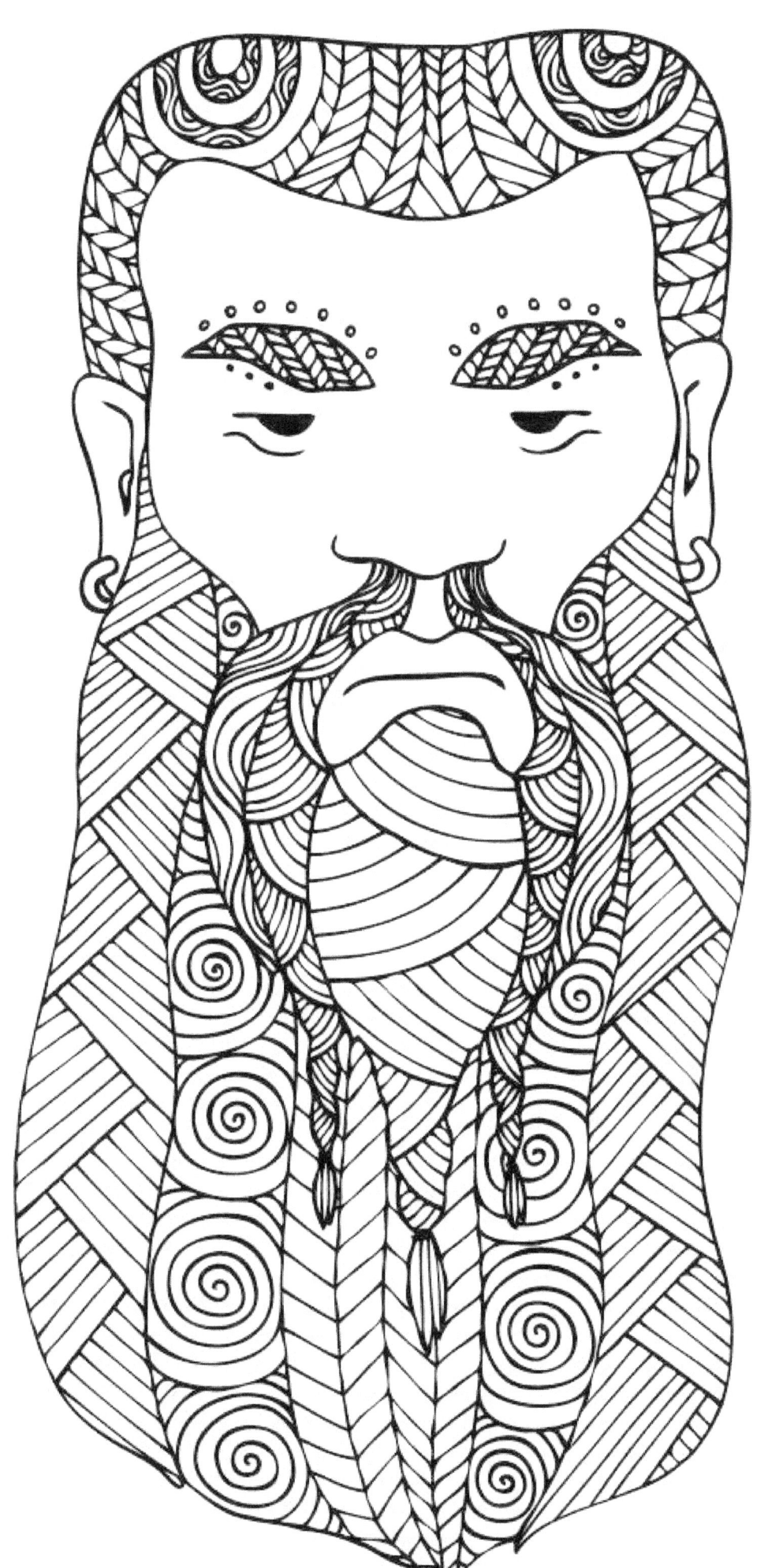

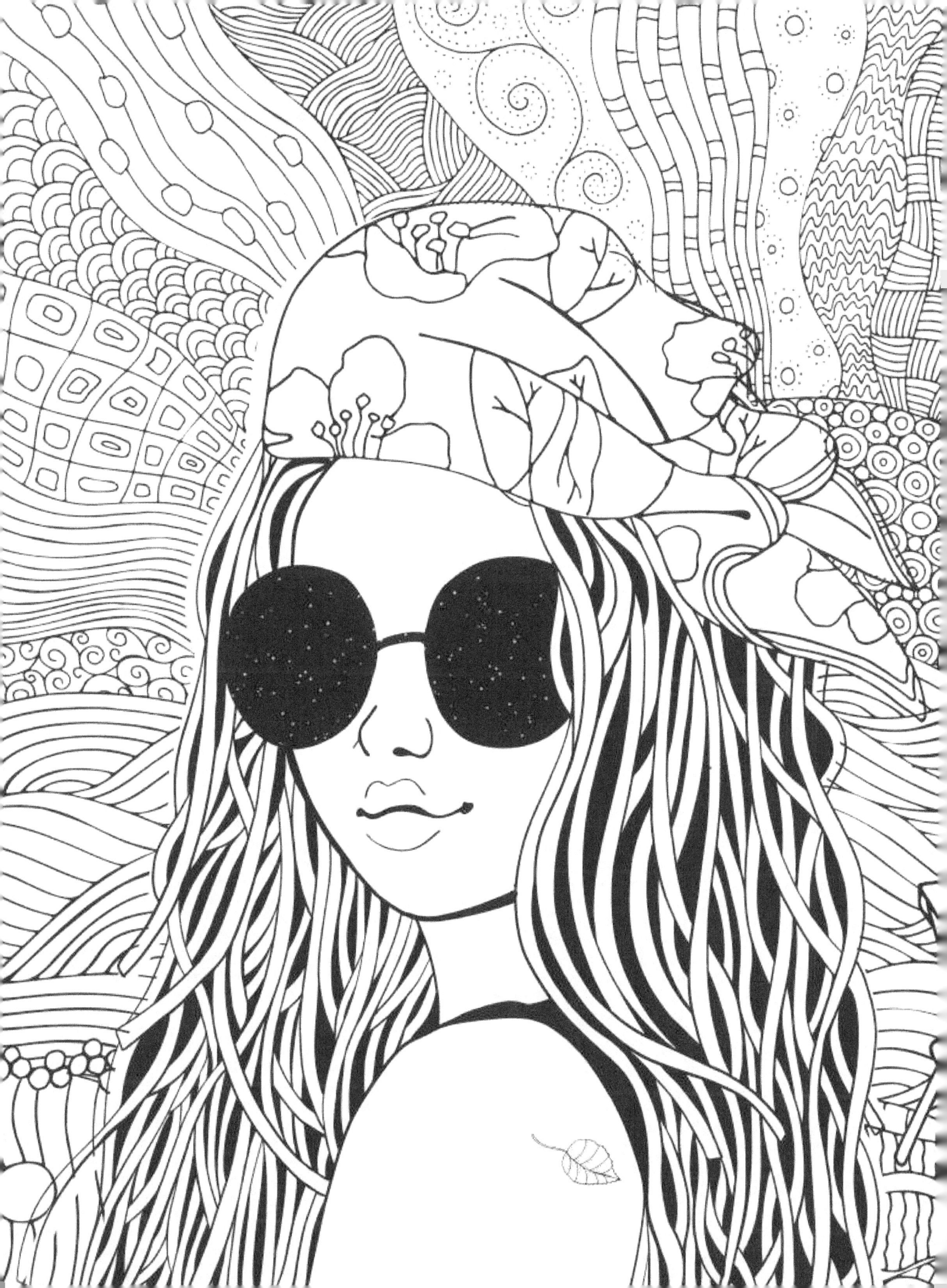

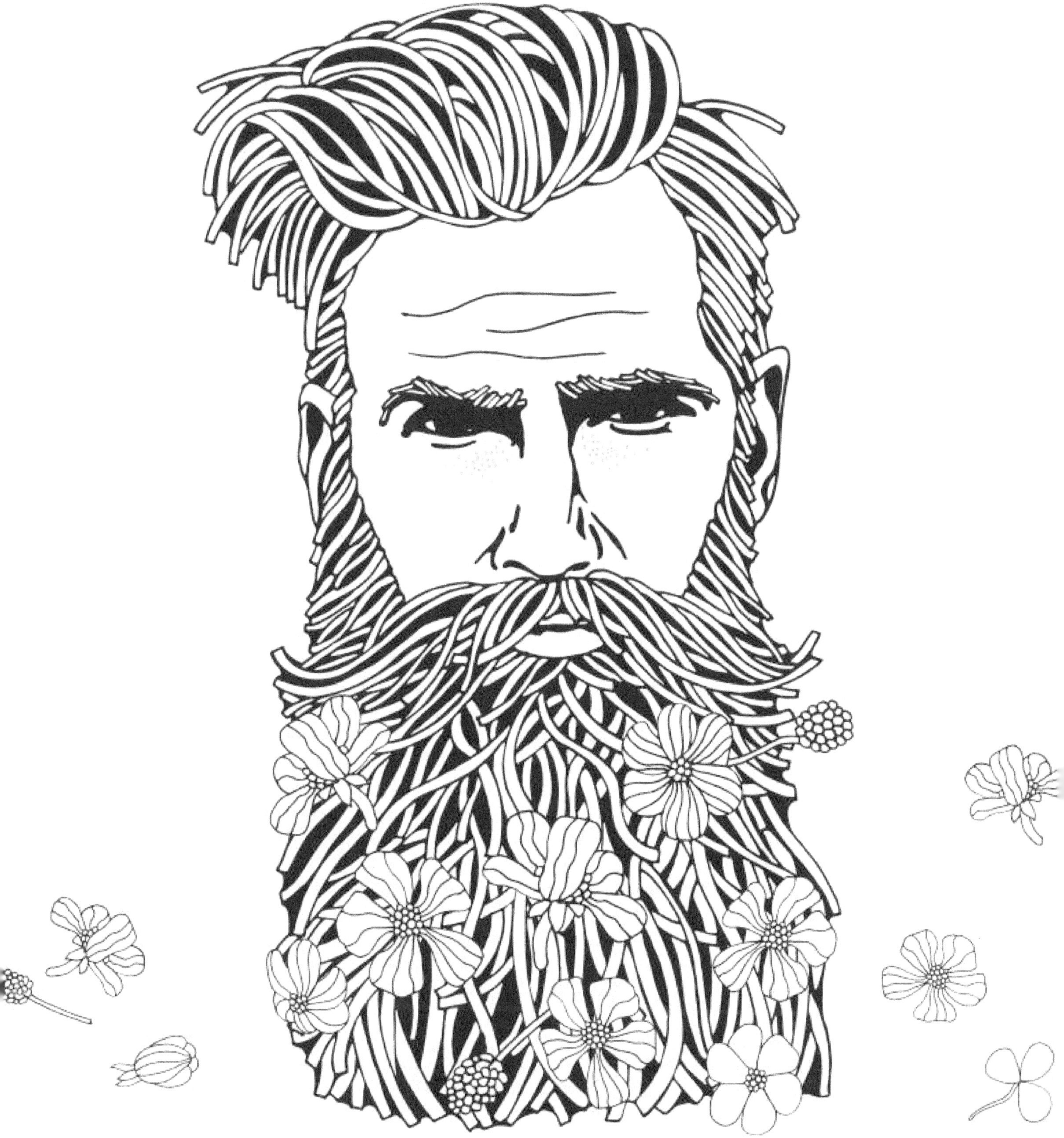

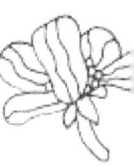
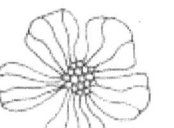
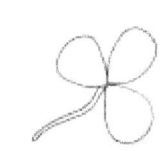

www.ingramcontent.com/pod-product-compliance
Lightning Source LLC
Chambersburg PA
CBHW081232170526
45165CB00009B/3040